100 DESIGNS FOR A MODERN WORLD

100 DESIGNS FOR A MODERN WORLD

Introduction by Penny Sparke

Skira *Rizzoli*
NEW YORK

KRAVIS DESIGN CENTER

CONTENTS

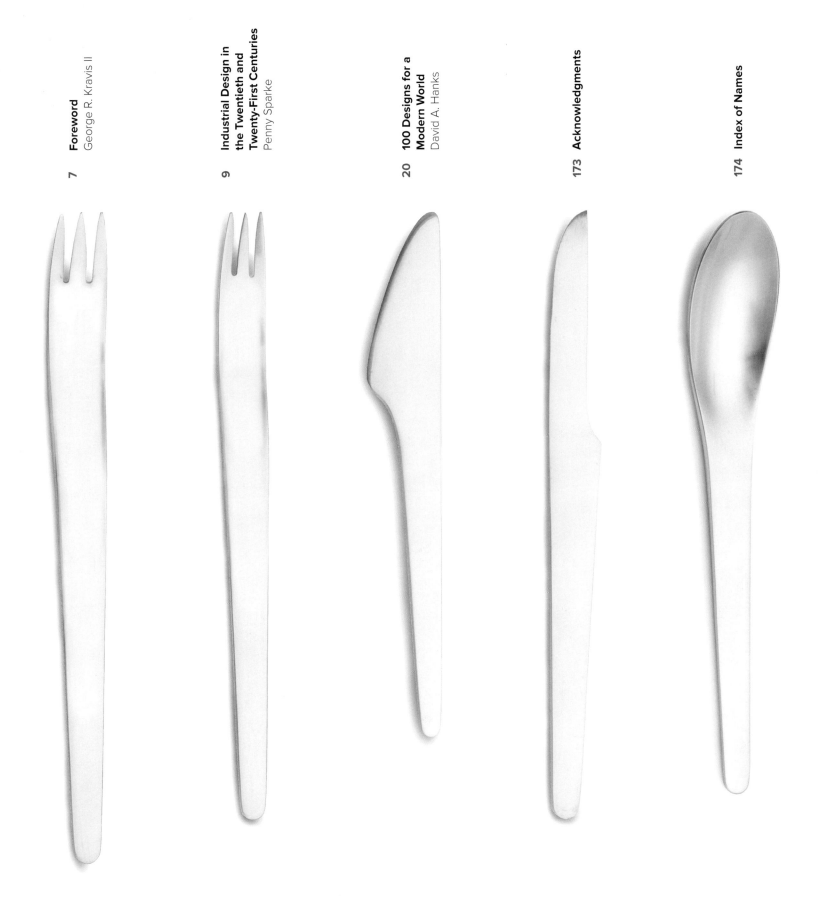

Foreword

Growing up in Tulsa, Oklahoma, I was fascinated by mechanical and electrical gadgets—anything with a cord, a plug, a battery, a light, a motor. These devices were my earliest introduction to design, particularly design developed for production, or industrial design. By 1949, when I was ten years old, I had acquired what proved to be the first piece in my collection, although I did not think of the RCA 45-rpm record changer, which had just come out, that way at the time. I liked the combination of the dark brown Bakelite and the gilt spindle with the red plastic top; I liked that it was compact and clean-lined; and I liked that, at $12.95, I could afford it.

Starting in the early 1960s, and throughout my twenty-five years in the broadcasting business, I collected modern consumer products, particularly radios and related electronic equipment. Then, in 2002, an exhibition organized by the Metropolitan Museum of Art—*American Modern, 1925–1940: Design for a New Age*—came to Tulsa. The display inspired me to collect designs from this key period. In 2008, I expanded the scope of my collection yet again, setting a goal of securing the best of industrial design, American and international, from 1900 to the present. Certain objects required great effort, such as the round *Ekco* radio. I had long been in possession of a black Bakelite version, but when I heard that a rare green example was for sale in London, I immediately boarded a plane to meet the collector. In purchasing an example of Noguchi's *Radio Nurse*—the only one known to be accompanied by its original box—I bid against at least one museum.

A particular strength of my collection is American design between 1930 and 1960, and many of my acquisitions fit into that category—appliances, electronics, and radios especially. Although thousands of these sorts of items are available, I'm looking for the best quality, both in condition and in aesthetics. I search for objects that are visually striking and important in the history of design. I visit museums all over the world to see existing collections. I'm most interested in objects that *look* modern—clean lines, undecorated, and inherently beautiful.

Sharing my collection with others has always been a pleasure; more recently, it has become my mission. I have lent and donated important design objects to the Museum of Modern Art, the Cooper Hewitt, the Indianapolis Museum of Art, and other institutions. In 2013, I established the Kravis Design Center. A new facility in Tulsa, which houses the two thousand–plus objects in my collection, was completed in 2015. This book celebrates the new gallery as well as the collection as a whole and fulfills my mission to share the objects and to invite everyone to enjoy the pleasures of design.

George R. Kravis II

Industrial Design in the Twentieth and Twenty-First Centuries

Penny Sparke

A new craftsmanship of the Machine Age is in existence, aiming again at rightness in things . . . the task confronting us is enormous—the design and construction, almost from scratch, of an environment in which human life can flourish as it should.

—Walter Dorwin Teague, *Design This Day: The Technique of Order in the Machine Age*, 1940

How often do we give a second thought to the objects that fill our homes, our workplaces, our leisure spaces, our streets and highways? From kettles to computers, electric fans to electronic tablets, and scooters to space shuttles, the objects of daily life sit quietly in our kitchens and on our desks, or transport us from place to place, while we barely acknowledge their existence. Most observers don't realize that someone has consciously selected their materials and deliberately given them their unique and often beautiful forms, always with an eye toward manufacture, often on a large scale; they exist simply as silent servants. However, these seemingly banal products can tell us fascinating stories. They have witnessed the dramatic shift from the mechanical to the digital world, and they are key symbols of the modern age, crucial pointers to the future, and a continual reminder that we live in a world defined largely by technology.

The changes that have occurred since the early 1900s in the design of the vacuum cleaner show how industrially manufactured products have evolved in the hands of designers. Created at the turn of the twentieth century as an improvement on the carpet sweeper—itself a development of the simple long-handled brush—the suction sweeper, as it was called then, comprised a number of disparate elements: a stick to hold, a brush to sweep, an electric motor to drive the suction, and a bag to contain the dust. With the addition of a streamlined plastic body/shell to conceal its inner workings, the vacuum cleaner finally emerged, in the 1930s, as a unified product with a sleek, stylish identity, an aerodynamic form that promised to sweep your carpets faster than ever before. It transformed what had once been a

Vacuum cleaner, 1908, produced by Suction Sweeper Co., New Berlin, Ohio

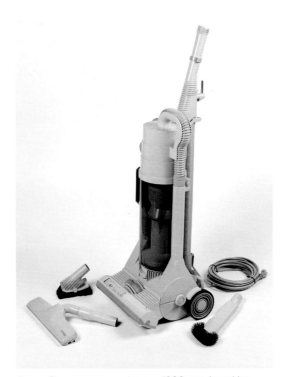

James Dyson, vacuum cleaner, 1986, produced by APEX, Inc., Tokyo, Japan

chore for the servant into a fun activity for the housewife. Six decades later, the English inventor-designer James Dyson devised a new method of mechanized sweeping that no longer required a bag. He also added a fresh range of colors—from pink to purple to yellow—to the hitherto dull machine, proving that designers continue to innovate even when a product performs its function adequately.

Indeed, most products that are designed to be fabricated in any quantity continue to be modified in response to our need to be more and more efficient and, perhaps even more important, to our unquenchable thirst for visual stimulation. These articles are the result of the creativity of many gifted designers, and the need to keep developing products is a response to their curiosity combined with technological innovation, changes in taste, and the need to keep the economy moving.

Art and Industry, 1900–1940

The redesign of the vacuum cleaner was the result of the marriage between art and industry that began at the end of the nineteenth century, a marriage that different countries interpreted in different ways. Various artists, architects, and manufacturers in Europe and the United States engaged in collaborations that led to the emergence of what we now call "industrial design"—that is, designing larger numbers of better products at lower prices. The challenges, both technological and aesthetic, of new materials have likewise provoked responses from industrial designers. In addition to various forms of processed wood, metals of the industrial age—including steel and aluminum—processed glass, modern plastics, and most recently, carbon fiber have led to many hitherto unimagined forms.

The United Kingdom was the first country to industrialize, and a few of its early manufacturers—the ceramics firm Wedgwood, for instance—worked with artists to make their products both look more attractive and address particular markets. By the 1860s, however, many British artists and architects had expressed their distaste for what they saw as the vulgar forms manufactured articles had taken on. Led by William Morris, these artists encouraged a return to the values of craftsmanship, and thereby temporarily halted the emergence of a modern industrial design movement. However, a number of Britain's industrial designers—Christopher Dresser in the nineteenth century and Wells Coates, Serge Chermayeff, and Christian Barman by the 1930s—became pioneering figures in the field. They collaborated happily with the manufacturing industry and generated innovative forms for its mass-produced goods.

Continental Europe also rose to the challenge. In Austria, artists and architects linked to the Wiener Werkstätte began to work with manufacturers. Germany, although it industrialized later than the United Kingdom, was very quick to embrace, and more willing than Britain to sustain, the union of art and industry. The German architect and graphic designer Peter Behrens created a complete visual identity—from sales brochures to kettles to fans to the factory building itself—for Allgemeine-Elektrizitäts-Gesellschaft (AEG), and the Deutscher Werkbund was formed in 1907 to provide support for the country's new, rational approach to the design of everyday industrial objects. The most radical design education establishment of the day, the Bauhaus, was formed in Weimar in 1919. It was hugely influential in promulgating the idea that architects should apply their ideas to furniture and other mass-produced artifacts. Building on ideas that had been developed by progressive artists in the Netherlands and the USSR, Bauhaus designers worked in a modern, geometric, machine-inspired style. These efforts resulted in some of the twentieth century's best-loved iconic designs, such as Marcel Breuer's *B3* club chair, or "Wassily."

Following in the wake of Germany, the Scandinavian countries—Sweden, Denmark, and Finland—devoted themselves to fashioning a softer model of industrial design, or "applied art," focused on craft-based makers of glass, ceramics, and furniture. The Finnish glassworks littala invited collaboration from artists Simon Gate and Edward Hald, while Swedish ceramics manufacturer Gustavsberg worked with Wilhelm Kåge on a number of influential modern designs. Finnish architect Alvar Aalto designed several furniture items made of bent plywood—in Germany, the material might have been tubular steel—while the Dane Poul Henningsen produced innovative light fixtures for Louis Poulsen.

Several other European countries embraced variants of the modern style in their industrial products of the interwar years. In addition to its pioneering work in poster design, France developed a decorative approach—known internationally as Art Deco—which was revealed at the 1925 Exposition Internationale des Arts Décoratifs et Industriels Modernes. Large exhibitions and world's fairs have also played an important role in spreading ideas about industrial design to an international audience. Important events of the twentieth century have included the exhibition *Machine Art* at New York's Museum of Modern Art in 1934; the New York World's Fair of 1939–1940; the "Good Design" installations at the Museum of Modern Art in the early 1950s; the Festival of Britain of 1951; Expo 67 in Montreal; and the Milan Triennales, which were initiated during the interwar years of the twentieth century and continue to the present.

Marcel Breuer, *B3* club chair, 1927–1928, produced by Standard Möbel, Berlin, Germany

Ralph Tubbs, Dome of Discovery, 1951, Festival of Britain, London, England

Expo 67 postcard showing R. Buckminster Fuller's geodesic dome for the American Pavilion, Montreal

Also playing a key role in disseminating the dominant industrial design ideas of the day and preparing designers for their roles in industry has been design education. Among the most influential institutions that have drawn on the work of the Bauhaus are the Art Center (today Art Center College of Design) in Pasadena, California, formed in 1930; Cranbrook Academy of Art in Bloomfield Hills, Michigan, established in 1932; Design Academy Eindhoven in the Netherlands, set up in 1947; Germany's Hochschule für Gestaltung, formed in 1951; the Royal College of Art in London, opened in 1837 (but most prominent from the 1950s onward); and Stanford University's D.School in California, created in 2004.

Art and Commerce in the United States, 1930–1940

The 1930s was, arguably, the heroic period for industrial design, a time when design was thought to align most closely with the spirit of the modern age. In addition to a consolidation of the industrial design profession, the decade saw a unique combination of economic, technological, and aesthetic factors that facilitated original collaborations between art and industry. These, in turn, led to the creation of both new consumer machines, such as office duplicators, and newly styled, more traditional products, such as ceramic and glass objects, made by established decorative arts manufacturers. These items were designed by a leading-edge generation of entrepreneurial individuals who took industrial design into a different era. With backgrounds in set design and commercial art, Walter Dorwin Teague, Norman Bel Geddes, Raymond Loewy, Henry Dreyfuss, and Harold Van Doren, in addition to others working in the more traditional manufacturing sector, including Russel Wright, Gilbert Rohde, and Kem Weber, applied their visualizing skills to a wide range of objects, transforming the everyday environment in the process.

The need for a continual redesign of existing industrial goods had been promoted in the late 1920s by Alfred P. Sloan of General Motors. He understood that design possessed the power to keep the economy moving, and he hired Hollywood set designer Harley Earl to create some exciting and up-to-date designs. Industrial design consulting, which emerged as a profession as other manufacturers followed Sloan's lead, contributed to the development of a novel product aesthetic rooted in a combination of the popular language of streamlining, with its origins in aerodynamics, and European Art Deco. The new goods became symbols of a world defined by modernity and consumption; they also, in certain settings, reflected a glamour that contrasted with the hardship of the Depression era. New machines for the home, the office, and

Harley Earl, *Y-Job*, 1939, produced by Buick, Flint, Michigan

the cocktail lounge, as well as countless objects of transportation, rolled off production lines, as did numerous redesigned articles for the so-called decorative arts industries—furniture, ceramics, glass, metalwork, and textiles among them.

The emergence and rise to fame of the designer for industry is one of the key stories of the modern age. Among the many who followed the American pioneers were the scrupulous German Dieter Rams, the radical Italian Ettore Sottsass, and the flamboyant Frenchman Philippe Starck. However, many less celebrated individuals have also played important roles in bringing designed products to people across the globe, whether as independent consultants or as full-time employees of large corporations. Not every designed object has a prominent name attached to it. Indeed, many of the most important industrial designs are anonymous, humble tools that, styled appropriately, inhabit the everyday world, performing their function effectively and enhancing lives in a quiet, understated way.

William Lansing Plum, *QT-50* radio cassette recorder, 1985, produced by Sharp Electronics Corp., Osaka, Japan

Industrial Design and the Modern Consumer, 1940–1980

Designers and manufacturers cannot work in isolation. Without consumers and users the cycle of designed products would be incomplete. As Josiah Wedgwood understood, and as Depression America very quickly learned, the addition of "art" to "industry" is necessary both in periods of economic expansion, which bring with them enhanced social mobility and the need for more choices, and in periods of tight finances, as design provides added value and differentiation. In the years after 1945, the expansion of the European economy encouraged many manufacturers to develop their own versions of industrial design as a means of stimulating consumer demand.

Starting in the 1950s, the streamlined aesthetic of interwar products was replaced by various modern industrial design languages. These included the "midcentury modern" look, manifest in decorative arts products and domestic interiors in the 1950s, and the Germanic neomodernist minimal look, which from the 1960s onward defined the "high-tech" appearance of countless machines, from hi-fi equipment to food mixers. The 1990s saw the reemergence of Germanic minimalism, first in interiors and furniture, and soon in electronic goods as well.

Another aesthetic to emerge at this time was inspired by postmodernist stylistic pluralism, by fun and nostalgia. It was evident in the "pink goods" produced in Japan in the 1980s by Sharp and others; in James Dyson's vacuum cleaners of the 1990s; in Jonathan Ive's jewellike *iMac* computer for Apple of 1998; and in the American Michael Graves's wide-ranging designs of the final decades of the twentieth century.

Several countries contributed to these postwar developments. It was in the United States that the model of midcentury modern first emerged. Presented at the "Good Design" exhibitions held at the Museum of Modern Art in the 1950s, it was driven by the designers Charles and Ray Eames, Alexander Girard, Eero Saarinen, Harry Bertoia, and George Nelson, working for Herman Miller and Knoll, among other companies. The new style was quickly emulated in Europe. In Britain, the "contemporary" style, exhibited in the work of Ernest Race and Robin Day, owed much to the United States. British design in this era was influenced by Scandinavia as well, where the emphasis was also on the home and on mass-produced goods with a decorative arts lineage. Danish furniture designers, including Hans Wegner, Arne Jacobsen, and Verner Panton, came to the fore at this time, while Finnish glass acquired a fresh exuberance in the hands of Tapio Wirkkala and others.

Germany took a slightly different route, focusing on a revival of the Bauhaus approach of the prewar years and adapting that aesthetic to appliances as well as to the products of the decorative arts industries. The notion of "Gute Form" (good form) grew out of the minimalist work of Dieter Rams, notably his designs for the Braun company, while the Hochschule Ulm also looked back to Bauhaus ideas.

Italian industrial design began to be recognized and admired internationally in the 1950s. The hugely innovative work that emerged from Italy, which embraced both furniture and domestic machines, was the product of collaborations between Italian architect-designers and the country's high-end, small-scale furniture makers and product manufacturers—Cassina, Artemide, Arteluce, Brionvega, and Olivetti among them. Italy's designers—Giò Ponti, the Castiglioni brothers, Vico Magistretti, Ettore Sottsass, Marco Zanuso, Joe Colombo, Richard Sapper, Mario Bellini, and others—used a range of new materials, from chromed steel to plastics, to create an aesthetic of "modern luxury."

The 1960s witnessed a reaction to the refined nature of much of Italy's industrial design output, however. Sottsass and others initiated an "anti-design" movement that, by the 1980s, had combined with postmodernism to undermine the international dominance of Germanic Gute Form and what many designers

Jonathan Ive and Apple Design Team, *iMac*, 1998, produced by Apple Computer, Inc., Cupertino, California

Achille and Pier Giacomo Castiglioni, *Taccia* table lamp, 1962, produced by Flos, Bovezzo, Italy

Front Design, *Sketch Furniture*, 2005, process
demonstrated by Acron Formservice AB,
Anderstorp, Sweden

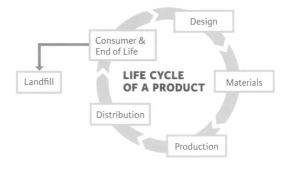

Eileen MacAvery Kane, sustainable design graphic
created for *Ethics: A Graphic Designer's Field Guide*, 2010

considered industry's excessive control over their work. The 1981 Memphis exhibit in Milan represented a key moment in that dramatic about-face, bringing together designers from a number of different countries. The same irreverent attitude would surface again in the work of Philippe Starck; of Ron Arad and Tom Dixon in Britain; of Frank Gehry in the United States; and of the Droog group in the Netherlands.

By the 1970s, Japan had also become a contender for leadership in the field of industrial design (or "product design," as it was being called). A group of Japanese designers was responsible for a new design direction that emphasized the impact of high technology, especially electronics and the possibilities of miniaturization, on the nature and appearance of a range of highly sophisticated products, from cameras to calculators to hi-fi systems. The Japanese high-tech product designers were mostly in-house employees, their names concealed behind the more familiar brands of large-scale manufacturing companies such as Sony, Sharp, and Toyota. This course combined the German minimalist style with visual displays of virtuosity, such as the use of complex control systems. At the same time, however, another circle of Japanese designers, including Sori Yanagi, Shiro Kuramata, Shigeru Uchida, and Masanori Umeda, was well known in the global design community. They developed a different approach, one that focused on furniture and on bringing together indigenous ideas about craft with progressive, international tendencies from within the discipline.

Global Industrial Design, 1980–Present

In the years since 1980, industrial design has become integrated into global economics and culture. So strong are the forces of pluralism and diversity that it is hard to identify national visual characteristics or single trends. Product design finally broke completely free from its links with craft, its need for stylistic unity, and the requirement that it represent only the present and the future. Designers felt free to look at the past and integrate historic references into their work. The late twentieth and early twenty-first centuries have witnessed both a rejection of Bauhaus rules and a renewal of the minimalist aesthetic that emerged from the school. In addition, sophisticated production technologies, which by the early 2000s include rapid prototyping and three-dimensional modeling, have introduced new freedoms into the scale of manufacturing and the visual possibilities of products.

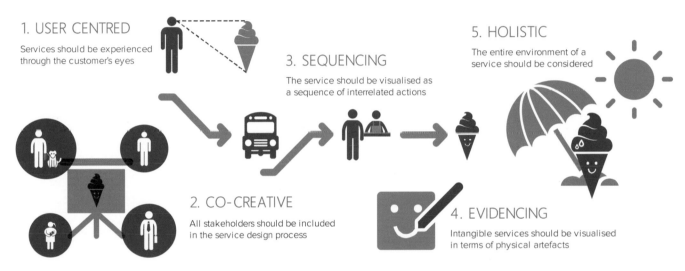

Matthew Tyas, *The Five Principles of Service Design Thinking*, 2011, designed for the first Global Service Jam

The period has also seen designers becoming increasingly focused on issues relating to the environment and on service and virtual design; in fact, in certain contexts, the idea of the object has become secondary. In the early twenty-first century this preoccupation has been reinforced by the many designers who are attempting to confront the multiple challenges of the era and who have become particularly interested in new ways of working, whether "co-design," "participatory design," or "social design." As a result, the celebrity designer and the iconic object have become less and less dominant. As the century progresses, designers are less concerned with a role as the glue between art and industry. Instead, these creative professionals, like those in numerous other disciplines, are increasingly conscious of the broader role they can play—some would say, they must play—in the world of today.

100 DESIGNS FOR

A MODERN WORLD

Koloman Moser
(1868–1918)
Jutta Sika
(1877–1964)
Plate, cup,
and saucer
Designed 1901–1902

Enameled porcelain, enamel
Plate diameter: 7⅜ inches (18.7 cm)
Produced by Josef Böck Wiener
Porzellanmanufaktur, Vienna, Austria
K2008.348.1–3

Peter Behrens
(1868–1940)
Electric kettle
Designed 1909

Nickel-plated brass, rattan
9 × 8¾ × 6¼ inches (22.9 × 22.2 × 15.9 cm)
Produced by Allgemeine-Elektritzitäts-
Gesellschaft (AEG), Berlin, Germany
K2010.23

Considered the world's first industrial designer, Peter Behrens trained as an artist in his native Hamburg. He was one of the founders of the Deutscher Werkbund, established in 1907 to improve the design of industrial products. That same year, he was hired as a consultant for the industrial and power concern AEG in Berlin. His work, which included the logo, advertising, products, and even the famous turbine factory, is considered one of the first comprehensive corporate identities. His electric teapots for AEG, composed of interchangeable elements for ease of mass production, were available in three simple, undecorated forms and three finishes.

Peter Behrens, AEG turbine factory, 1908–1909, Berlin, Germany

STAATLICHES
BAUHAUS
IN WEIMAR
1919-1923

Herbert Bayer
(1900–1985)
László Moholy-Nagy
(1895–1946)
*Staatliches Bauhaus
in Weimar 1919–1923*
exhibition catalogue
Published 1923

Letterpress, lithograph
9⅞ × 10 inches (25.1 × 25.5 cm)
Published by Bauhaus Verlag,
Weimar, Germany
K2011.204

László Moholy-Nagy, title page of *Staatliches Bauhaus in Weimar 1919–1923*

Josef Hartwig, master of the Bauhaus sculpture workshop from 1921 to 1925, created a modern version of the ancient game of chess as a design for production. The shape of each piece is a cube refashioned to correspond to its prescribed style of movement. The king, which moves one square in any direction, is a cube topped with another cube. The knight suggests the right angle direction of its L-shaped course. The bishop's cross form signals its diagonal moves. The chess set epitomizes Bauhaus principles, which fuse abstract geometric elements with functionalism.

Joost Schmidt, instructions for Hartwig chess set

Designer unknown
Pencil sharpener
Designed after 1925

Bakelite, steel
4 × 4½ × 2 inches (10.2 × 11.4 × 5.1 cm)
Produced by Garant, Czechoslovakia
K2008.193

Poul Henningsen
(1894–1967)
PH table lamp
Designed c. 1927

Glass, brass, Bakelite
20¼ × 15½ × 15½ inches
(51.5 × 39.5 × 39.5 cm)
Produced by Louis Poulsen & Co.,
Copenhagen, Denmark
K2010.343

Jean G. Theobald
(1873–1952)
Dinette set, model 7036
Designed 1928
(design patent D76,564)

Silverplate, wood
3½ × 8½ × 8½ inches (8.9 × 21.6 × 21.6 cm)
Produced by Wilcox Silver Plate Company/
International Silver Company,
Meriden, Connecticut
K2010.65

The daughter of a Budapest silversmith, Ilonka Karasz
was one of the first women to study at the city's Royal
Academy of Arts and Crafts. In 1913, she immigrated to
New York City, where she designed modern furniture,
textiles, and metalwork that demonstrate the influence of
the Dutch De Stijl movement. Her multifaceted career
included 186 covers for the *New Yorker*, beginning in
1924, and illustrations for other magazines. Her diminutive
sugar bowl and creamer, bold and geometric, recall
designs from the Bauhaus metal workshops in Weimar
and Dessau, Germany.

Ilonka Karasz
(1896–1981)
Sugar bowl and creamer
Designed c. 1928

Electroplated nickel silver
Sugar bowl: 3 × 5⅜ × 4⅜ inches
(7.5 × 13.7 × 11 cm)
Produced by Paye and Baker Manufacturing
Company, North Attleboro, Massachusetts
Cooper Hewitt, Smithsonian Design Museum,
gift of George R. Kravis II, 2013-54-2/3

Paul T. Frankl
(1887–1958)
Clock
Designed c. 1928

Bakelite, brushed-burnished silver,
chromium-plated and enameled metal
7¾ × 5¾ × 3¾ inches (19.7 × 14.6 × 9.5 cm)
Produced by Warren Telechron Company,
Ashland, Massachusetts
K2008.153

Reuben Haley
(1872–1933)
Two *Ruba Rombic* vases
and decanter
Designed c. 1928 (design
patent D74,881–74,882)

Glass
Tallest vase: 9¼ × 8 × 8 inches
(23.7 × 20.2 × 20.2 cm)
Produced by Consolidated Lamp and
Glass Company, Art Glassware Division,
Coraopolis, Pennsylvania
K2013.7.1, K2008.149, K2010.113

Jacob Jongert
(1883–1942)
Coffee and tea box
Designed c. 1928–1930

Enameled tin
16½ × 11¾ × 14⅜ inches
(41.9 × 29.8 × 36.5 cm)
Produced by Wed. J. Bekkers & Zoon,
Dordrecht, for Van Nelle,
Rotterdam, Netherlands
K2011.205

Richard Schadewell
Telephone
Designed 1929

Bakelite, nickel-plated brass,
enameled metal
5¼ × 9⅝ × 6 inches (13.5 × 24.5 × 15.3 cm)
Produced by Telefonbau & Normalzeit
GmbH (formerly Fuld & Co.),
Frankfurt, Germany
K2013.134

George Sakier
(1897–1988)
Three *Lotus* vases
Designed 1929–1938

Glass
Tallest vase: 12¾ × 4¾ × 4¾ inches
(32.4 × 12 × 12 cm)
Produced by Fostoria Glass Company,
Moundsville, West Virginia
K2012.167.1–3

Designer unknown
Toaster
Designed c. 1930

Chromium-plated steel, Bakelite, ceramic
9½ × 9 × 6 inches (24.1 × 22.9 × 15.2 cm)
Produced by Saluta, Germany
K2008.162

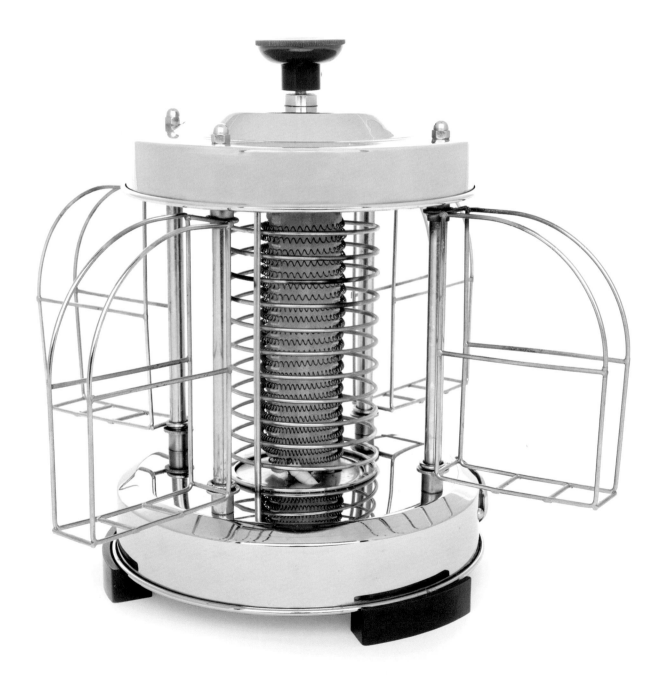

George Sakier
(1897–1988)
Sink with stand
Designed c. 1930
(stand, design patent
D85,060)

Porcelain, chromium-plated steel
34 × 29 × 19½ inches
(86.4 × 73.7 × 49.5 cm)
Produced by American Radiator and
Standard Sanitary Corporation,
New York, New York
K2008.147

Illustration, *Arts & Decoration*, November 1933

Designer unknown
Roller bearing
Designed c. 1930–1950

Steel, brass
9 × 9 × 2 inches (23 × 6.2 × 6.2 cm)
Manufacturer unknown
K2012.28

Amelia Earhart, John Dewey, and Charles R. Richards, judges for the most beautiful objects from the *Machine Art* exhibition with first, second, and third prize winners, 1934, Museum of Modern Art, New York

Hans Luckhardt
(1890–1954)
Wassili Luckhardt
(1899–1972)
ST14 folding side chair
Designed 1931

Chromium-plated steel, ash plywood
34⅝ × 21⅛ × 24¼ inches
(88 × 53.8 × 61.5 cm)
Produced by Gebrüder Thonet,
Vienna, Austria
K2011.203

A. M. (Adolphe Mouron)
Cassandre
(1901–1968)
Miniwatt/Philips
Radio poster
Designed 1931

Offset lithograph
22½ × 15¼ inches (57 × 38.5 cm)
Produced by Alliance Graphique,
Paris, France
K2011.96

Wells Coates
(1895–1958)
Ekco radio,
model AD65
Designed 1932

Bakelite, stainless steel, fabric
16 × 15½ × 8¼ inches (40.5 × 39.5 × 21 cm)
Produced by E. K. Cole & Co., Ltd.,
Southend-on-Sea, Essex, England
K2013.26

Designer unknown
Globe plumb bob
Designed c. 1934

Brass, steel
5¾ × 1⅛ × 1⅛ inches (14.6 × 3 × 3 cm)
Produced by Eugene Dietzgen Co.,
Chicago, Illinois
K2011.72

First used by ancient Egyptians in architecture, astronomy, and other pursuits, the plumb bob continues to ensure that contemporary constructions are perfectly vertical. This precision instrument exemplifies the industrial aesthetic admired by the Museum of Modern Art's first director, Alfred H. Barr, Jr. In the catalogue for the institution's 1934 exhibition *Machine Art*, he praised the "unintentional" beauty of industrial objects created "without benefit of artist-designer." This symmetrical plumb bob is crafted with an ingenious reversible tip: the sharp point can be flipped safely inside the bob to prevent damage and injuries.

Walter Dorwin Teague
(1883–1960)
Baby Brownie camera
Designed c. 1934

Bakelite, metal, glass
3⅛ × 3⅛ × 2⅞ inches (8 × 8.5 × 7.3 cm)
Produced by Eastman Kodak Company,
Rochester, New York
Cooper Hewitt, Smithsonian Design Museum,
gift of George R. Kravis II, 2014-25-4

Illustration showing *Baby Brownie* in open and closed positions, *Pencil Points*, September 1937

Gilbert Rohde
(1894–1944)
Z clock, model 4090
Designed c. 1934

Chromium-plated and enameled
brass, glass
12 × 12⅝ × 3½ inches (30.5 × 32 × 9 cm)
Produced by Herman Miller Clock Company,
Zeeland, Michigan
K2012.9

Walter Von Nessen
(1889–1943)
Table lamp
Designed c. 1935

Copper, steel
11½ × 9¼ × 8 inches
(29.2 × 23.5 × 20.3 cm)
Produced by Nessen Studio, Inc.,
New York, New York
K2008.216

Wilfred O. Langille
(1895–1996)
after a design by
Frederik Ljungström
Ribbonaire fan,
model 6-1
Designed c. 1935
(design patent D84,642)

Bakelite, ribbon
10 × 4½ × 7 inches (25.4 × 11.4 × 17.8 cm)
Produced by Diehl Manufacturing Co. for
Singer Sewing Machine Co.,
New York, New York
K2008.580

William Lescaze
(1896–1969)
Salt and pepper shakers
Designed c. 1935

Aluminum, steel
Each: 1¾ × 2 × ⅝ inches (4.4 × 5.1 × 1.6 cm)
Produced by Revere Copper and Brass
Company, Inc., Rome, New York
K2008.308

Henry Dreyfuss
(1904–1972)
Vacuum cleaner,
model 150
Designed c. 1935

Steel, enameled steel, aluminum,
canvas, rubber, Bakelite
48 × 12¾ × 14½ inches
(122 × 32.5 × 36.5 cm)
Produced by the Hoover Company,
North Canton, Ohio
K2012.30

Hoover Company advertisement, c. 1950

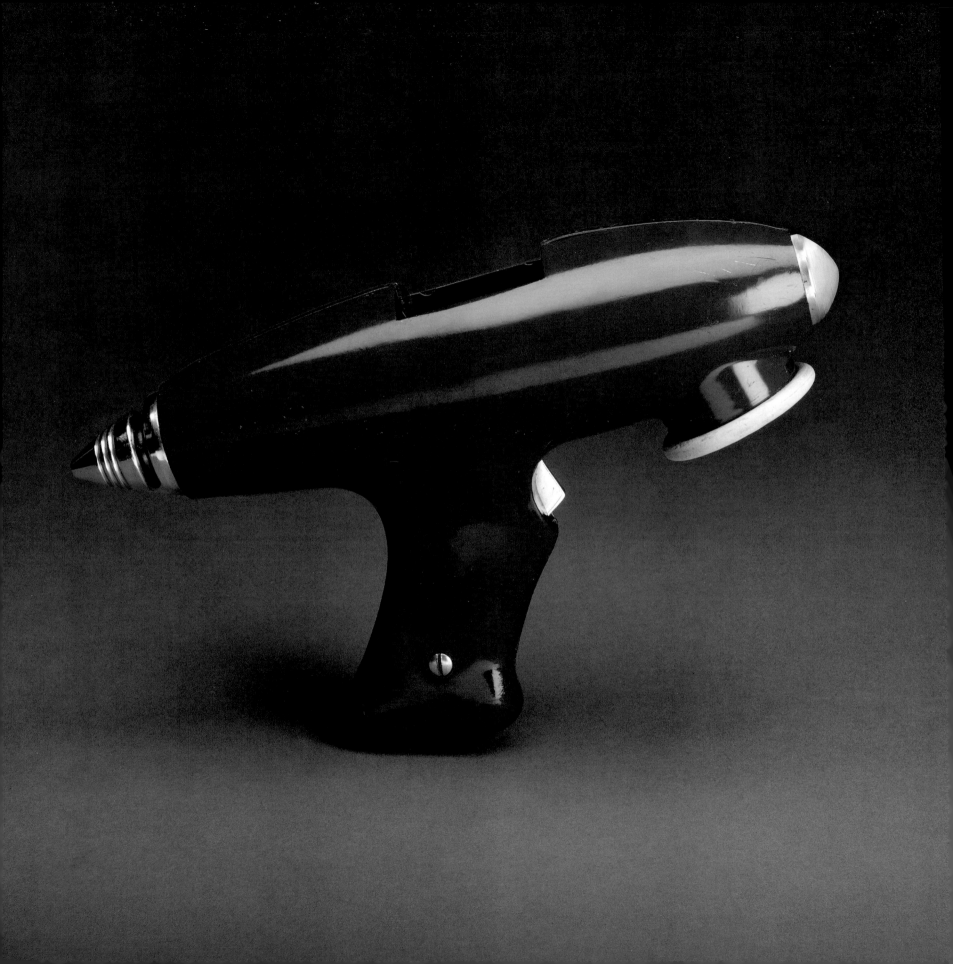

Designer unknown
Ice gun
Designed c. 1935

Enameled aluminum, chromium-plated
steel, rubber
6¾ × 11 × 2¾ inches (17.1 × 27.9 × 7 cm)
Produced by Opco Company,
Los Angeles, California
K2013.45

Russel Wright
(1904–1976)
Saturn punch bowl
with twelve cups and
cup tray
Designed c. 1935

Aluminum, walnut
Diameter: 18⅛ inches (46 cm)
Produced by Wright Accessories/Raymor,
New York, New York
K2008.179

Designer unknown
Toy racer, model BV-52
Designed 1935–1955

Enameled pewter, rubber
1½ × 7 × 2 inches (4 × 18 × 5 cm)
Produced by Barclay Manufacturing Co.,
North Bergen, New Jersey
K2010.302

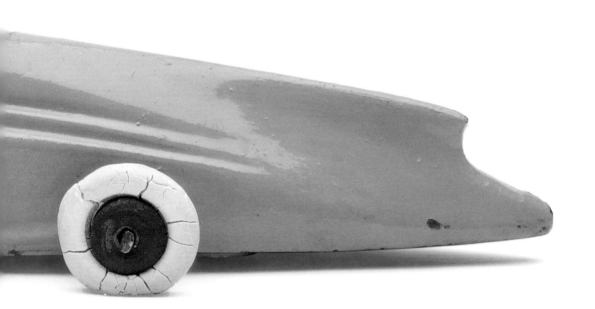

Alvar Aalto
(1898–1976)
Vase, model 3031
Designed 1936

Glass
11⅝ × 12⅜ × 11⅛ inches
(29.5 × 31.4 × 28.3 cm)
Produced by Karhula-Iittala Glassworks,
Iittala, Finland
K2009.19

John Gordon Rideout
(1898–1951)
Kettle, model 4133M
Designed 1936

Magnalite (aluminum, magnesium, and nickel alloy), ebonized wood
6⅞ × 9⅝ × 8⅝ inches (17.5 × 24.5 × 22 cm)
Produced by Wagner Manufacturing Company, Sidney, Ohio
K2012.139

Christian Barman
(1898–1980)
Iron
Designed 1936

Porcelain, chromium-plated cast iron,
phenol plastic
5 × 9 × 4½ inches (14.5 × 20 × 11.5 cm)
Produced by His Master's Voice,
London, England
K2010.1

Frederick Hurten Rhead
(1880–1942)
Two *Fiesta* pitchers
Designed c. 1936

Glazed earthenware
Large pitcher: 7¼ × 8 × 4½ inches
(18.5 × 20.3 × 11.5 cm)
Produced by Homer Laughlin China
Company, Newell, West Virginia
Cooper Hewitt, Smithsonian Design Museum,
2015-5-1/2, gift of George R. Kravis II

Brochure for *American Modern*
dinnerware, c. 1937

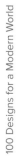

Russel Wright
(1904–1976)
Four *American
Modern* pitchers
Designed 1937

Glazed earthenware
Each: 10¾ × 8⅛ × 6½ inches
(27.3 × 20.6 × 16.5 cm)
Produced by Steubenville Pottery
Company, Steubenville, Ohio
K2008.103.1–4

René-André Coulon
(1908–1997)
Radiaver radiator
Designed 1937

Glass, steel, nickel
33 × 20 × 16¾ inches (50.7 × 42.5 × 13 cm)
Produced by Saint-Gobain Glass,
Courbevoie, France
K2011.147

In 1937, French architect and designer René-André Coulon collaborated with fellow architect Jacques Adnet to create a pavilion for the well-known glass manufacturer Saint-Gobain at the Paris International Exposition. The two architects introduced works of furniture in glass and metal; Coulon also presented what would become his most famous design, this inventive electric radiator, which is illuminated by a light source in the molded glass base. Made of metal heating strips within double plates of Saint-Gobain's trademarked tempered glass, Sekurit, the appliance exemplified a new concept in radiant heating for the modern interior, providing transparency and a sense of lightness.

Norman Bel Geddes
(1893–1958)
Worthen Paxton
(1905–1977)
Soda King siphon bottle
Designed c. 1938
(design patent D112,535)

Chromium-plated and enameled metal,
brass, rubber
10 × 4 × 4 inches (25.4 × 10.1 × 10.2 cm)
Produced by Walter Kidde Sales Company,
Bloomfield, New Jersey
K2008.225

Box for *Soda King* siphon

During the era of Prohibition, from 1920 to 1933, more and
more Americans adopted the habit of drinking at home.
New forms in accessories for mixed drinks emerged, such
as the rocketlike *Soda King*. Its spout and operating button
barely interrupt the continuous smooth contour; the stylish
silhouette and contrast between red-enameled top and
chromium body are markedly modern. Although the design
was patented by Worthen Paxton, an employee in Norman
Bel Geddes's office, the *Soda King* is clearly stamped with
the name of the firm's founder.

**Pittsburgh Plate
Glass Company
Design Department**
Armchair
Designed c. 1939

Glass, metal, fabric
29 × 22⅜ × 22½ inches (73.7 × 56.8 × 57.2 cm)
Produced c. 1947 for H. H. Turchin Company,
New York, New York
K2010.69

Dining room, Glass Center, New York World's Fair, 1939–1940, New York

Norman Bel Geddes
(1893–1958)
Patriot radio, model
FC-400
Designed 1940–1941

Catalin plastic
8 × 11 × 5½ inches (20.3 × 27.9 × 14 cm)
Produced by Emerson Radio and Phonograph
Corporation, New York, New York
K2008.197

Advertisement for Monsanto Plastics' *Opalon* showing *Patriot* radio

Arthur B. Peterson
Sander
Designed c. 1941
(design patent D130,772)

Aluminum
3 × 7 × 2⅛ inches (7.6 × 17.8 × 5.4 cm)
Produced by Behr-Manning, Troy, New York
K2011.60

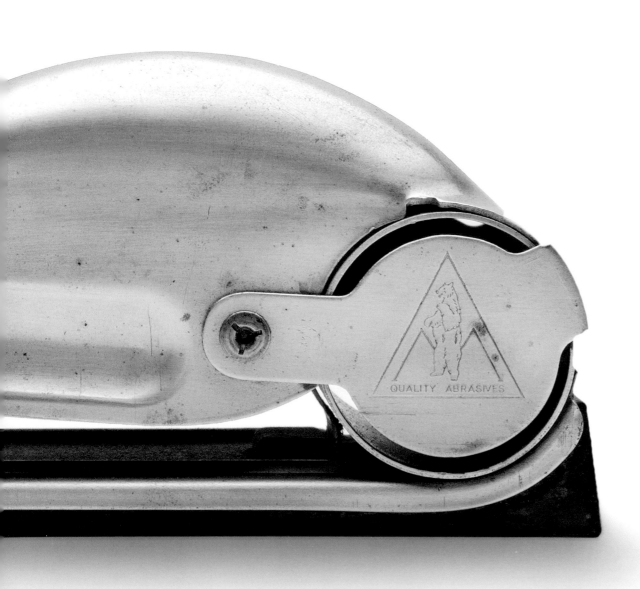

Jean Carlu
(1900–1997)
America's Answer!
Production poster
Designed 1942

Offset lithograph
30 × 40 inches (76.2 × 101.6 cm)
Produced by U.S. Government Printing Office,
Washington, D.C.
K2013.9

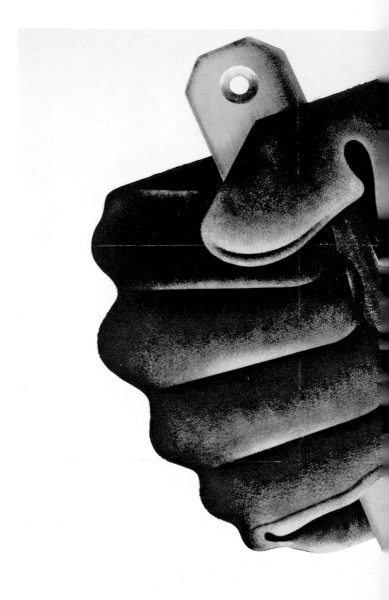

America's answer!

...ODUCTION

DIVISION OF INFORMATION
OFFICE FOR EMERGENCY MANAGEMENT
WASHINGTON, D.C.

Viktor Schreckengost
(1906–2008)
Two *Jiffy Ware* pitchers
Designed 1942

Glazed earthenware
Large pitcher: 6⅝ × 7¼ × 3⅝ inches
(16.8 × 18.4 × 9.2 cm)
Produced by American Limoges Company,
Sebring, Ohio
K2010.100.1–2

Brochure for *Jiffy Ware,* c. 1942

The *Jiffy Ware* pitcher exemplifies American streamlined design at its best. The horizontal "speed" lines at the base and spout suggest efficiency; indeed, a company brochure compared the pitchers to high-speed trains, planes, and automobiles. The foldout proclaimed that *Jiffy Ware* was "designed in the spirit of our times," that is, in keeping with the tenets of modernity. The flattened sides of the pitchers and other pieces in the line saved space when stored in modern refrigerators. Like *Fiesta* and other colorful earthenware, *Jiffy Ware* responded to the less formal American lifestyle that became common in the 1930s.

Designer unknown
Silver Streak iron
Designed 1943

Pyrex glass, chromium-plated cast iron,
aluminum, plastic
5⅝ × 3⅞ × 9½ inches (14.4 × 10 × 24 cm)
Produced by Corning Glass Works, Corning,
New York, and Saunders Machine & Tool
Corporation, Yonkers, New York
K2008.169

This iconic iron was named after the Chicago, Burlington
and Quincy Railroad's famous high-speed *Silver Streak
Zephyr* train, inaugurated in 1940. The body of the iron
consists of heat-resistant Pyrex glass, originally developed
for bakeware. This material selection responded to the
need during World War II to conserve metals for military
purposes. The ergonomic glass form was painted on the
interior in one of six brilliant colors. Corning provided the
glass components to Saunders, which mounted them on
metal bases. The iron did not go into production until 1946,
after the war ended.

André Mounique
Yves Jugeau
Jumo desk lamp
Designed 1945
(utility patent 2,543,926)

Bakelite, chromium-plated steel, copper
Fully extended: 20¼ × 7½ x 11 inches
(51.4 × 19.1 × 27.9 cm)
Produced by Société Nouvelle des
Établissements Jumo, Paris, France
K2008.623

Eva Zeisel
(1906–2011)
Town and Country salt
and pepper shakers
Designed c. 1945

Glazed earthenware
Salt: 4½ × 3 × 2¼ inches (11.5 × 7.7 × 5.8 cm)
Produced by Red Wing Potteries, Inc.,
Red Wing, Minnesota
K2008.256

Eero Saarinen
(1910–1961)
Grasshopper
lounge chair
Designed 1946

Birch plywood, upholstery
26¾ × 33 × 34¼ inches (67.9 × 83.8 × 87 cm)
Produced by Knoll Associates,
New York, New York
K2009.57

Living room, Wohnbedarf exhibition, c. 1957, Zurich, Switzerland

George Nelson & Associates
(active 1947–1983)
Stereo cabinet, model 4743
Designed 1946

Combed oak, lacquered wood, glass, plastic, linen, aluminum
38¼ × 92¼ × 19½ inches
(97.2 × 241.9 × 49.5 cm)
Produced by Herman Miller Furniture Company, Zeeland, Michigan
K2010.164

Living room showing an alternate configuration of the stereo cabinet

Benjamin Bowden
(1906–1998)
Spacelander bicycle
Designed 1946

Fiberglass, chromium-plated steel,
leather, rubber
41 × 72 × 23 inches (104.1 × 182.9 × 58.4 cm)
Produced by Bombard Industries,
Grand Haven, Michigan
K2013.44

Hans Bellmann
(1911–1990)
Occasional table,
model 103
Designed c. 1946

Laminated plywood, lacquered wood
21 × 23¾ × 23¾ inches (53.3 × 60.3 × 60.3 cm)
Produced by Knoll Associates,
New York, New York
K2012.227

114 Large tripod table, Hans Bellman design

Illustration from Knoll catalogue, 1950

Marshall M. Robinson
Photospot spotlight,
model V-31
Designed c. 1946
(design patent D146,809)

Enameled steel, Bakelite, aluminum, glass
12¼ × 12¼ × 9½ inches (31 × 31.5 × 24 cm)
Produced by National Instrument Corporation,
Houston, Texas
K2010.43

Tapio Wirkkala
(1915–1985)
Two vases, models
3213 and 3115
Designed 1947

Glass
Tall vase: 10¼ × 3 × 3 inches
(26 × 7.6 × 7.6 cm)
Produced by Karhula-Iittala Glassworks,
Iittala, Finland
K2009.48.1–2

Marjorie Tate
(1920–2015)
Leonard Tate
(1918–1987)
Betty Macaulay
Allen T. Macaulay
(1920–1994)
Plate, cup, and saucer
Designed c. 1947
(cup, design patent
D153,887)

Glazed earthenware
Plate: 10½ × 9 inches (26.7 × 22.9 cm)
Produced by Tamac, Inc., Perry, Oklahoma
K2008.129.1–3

Ernst Fischer
(1910–2006)
Freia portable electric
sewing machine
Designed 1948

Enameled steel, metal, Bakelite
Closed: 18 × 12 × 3⅜ inches (45.7 × 30.5 × 8.6 cm)
Open: 10⅛ × 34 × 12 inches (25.7 × 86.4 × 30.5 cm)
Produced by VEB Ernst-Thälmann-Werke,
Suhl, East Germany
Museum of Modern Art, 124.2010, gift of
George R. Kravis II

Charles Eames
(1907–1978)
Ray Eames
(1912–1988)
Armchair
Designed 1948–1950

Fiberglass-reinforced polyester, steel, wood
31¼ × 25 × 24½ inches (79.4 × 63.5 × 62.2 cm)
Produced by Zenith Plastics, Gardena, California,
for Herman Miller Furniture Company,
Zeeland, Michigan
K2008.334

Illustration from 1952 Herman Miller catalogue showing variations of the Eames plastic shell chair

Harry Mohr Weese
(1915–1998)
Baldry table lamp,
model 40
Designed 1949

Chromium-plated steel
14½ × 15 × 4½ inches (36.8 × 38.1 × 11.4 cm)
Produced for Baldwin Kingrey, Chicago, Illinois
K2011.46

Known for designing Washington, D.C.'s Metro stations in
the 1960s, Harry Weese studied architecture in the 1930s
at MIT and Cranbrook Academy of Art. In 1940, he started
an architecture practice in Chicago. The *Baldry* lamp
was developed for the modern design store he founded
in Chicago in 1947 with his wife, Kitty Baldwin, and Jody
Kingrey. *Baldry* was the name of Weese's line of furniture
and lamps produced in small quantities for Baldwin Kingrey.
Based on a 1940 lamp by Peter Pfisterer, this functional
design is composed of simple geometric elements: conical
lead-weighted base, cylindrical screw-on deflector, flexible
gooseneck shaft.

Charles Eames
(1907–1978)
Ray Eames
(1912–1988)
ETR coffee table
Designed 1950–1951

Plywood, plastic laminate, zinc
10 × 89 × 9¼ inches (25.4 × 226 × 74.3 cm)
Produced by Herman Miller Furniture Company,
Zeeland, Michigan
K2008.336

Charles Eames and Eero Saarinen, living room, Entenza House (Case Study House #9), Los Angeles, California, 1949

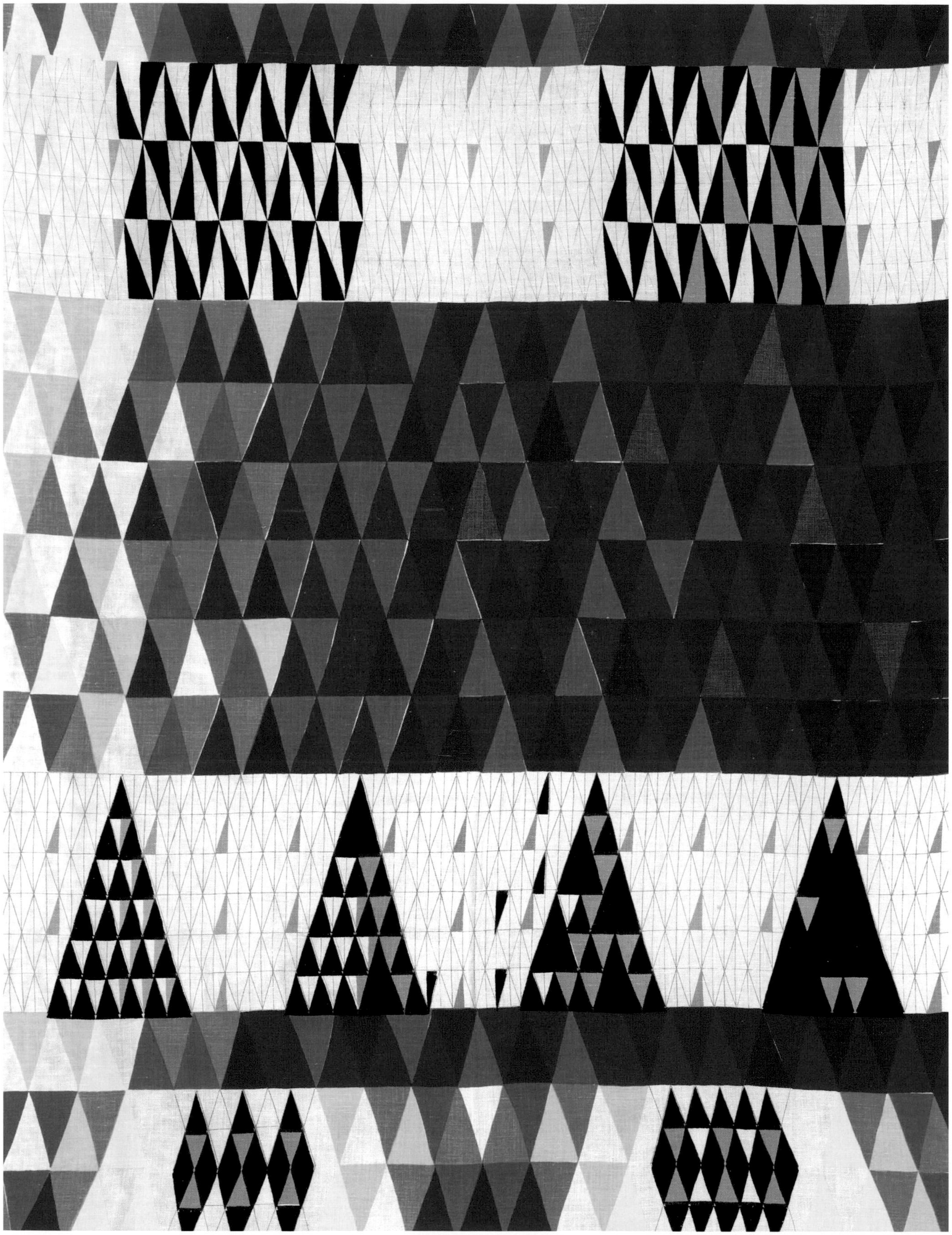

Sven Gottfrid Markelius
(1889–1972)
Pythagoras textile
Designed 1952

Printed linen
60 × 49½ inches (152.4 × 125.7 cm)
Produced by Knoll Textiles, Inc.,
New York, New York
K2013.25

Trained as an architect in Stockholm, Sven Markelius
was also recognized for town planning and fabric design.
The geometric grid of *Pythagoras* suggests an architectural
plan. Named for the Greek philosopher and mathematician,
the pattern uses alternating bands of triangles within a bold
color scheme. Originally created as a stage curtain for the
Folkets Hus (People's House) in Sweden, *Pythagoras* was
commercially produced in red, yellow, and blue colorways
by Nordiska Kompaniet in Stockholm and later by Knoll in
New York.

Herbert Krenchel
(1922–2014)
Six *Krenit* bowls
Designed 1953

Enameled steel
Largest bowl: 5¾ × 9¾ × 9¾ inches
(14.6 × 24.8 × 24.8 cm)
Produced by Torben Ørskov,
Espergærde, Denmark
K2008.122.1–6

George Nelson & Associates
(active 1947–1983)
Cone table clock
Designed 1954

Lacquered wood, enameled aluminum, enameled steel, plastic
6½ × 5¾ × 6 inches (16.6 × 14.6 × 15.5 cm)
Produced by Howard Miller Clock Company, Zeeland, Michigan
K2008.237

Architect George Nelson became the design director for the Herman Miller Furniture Company in 1946. Beginning in 1947, his office designed a series of modern clocks for the Howard Miller Clock Company, run by a Miller relative. Irving Harper, an associate in the Nelson office, developed many of the clocks. The timepieces have a whimsical quality that relates to midcentury modern sculpture—the works of Alexander Calder, Naum Gabo, and Barbara Hepworth, for instance—and treat geometric and functional Bauhaus precepts with humor. Following the principles of modern design, the clock faces were minimal, replacing the numbers with shapes, in this case, white map pins.

Sori Yanagi
(1915–2011)
Butterfly stool
Designed 1954

Rosewood, brass
15½ × 17⅜ × 12⅛ inches (39.4 × 44.1 × 30.8 cm)
Produced by Tendo Co., Ltd., Tendo, Japan
K2009.49

Designer unknown
Fan
Designed c. 1955

Melamine, vinyl, aluminum
5⅞ × 5⅛ × 6⅞ inches (15 × 13 × 17.5 cm)
Produced by E. Aghetto, Turin, Italy
K2010.34

Hans Gugelot
(1920–1965)
Dieter Rams
(born 1932)
Phonosuper SK5 radio
and record player
Designed 1956

Enameled metal, plywood, Plexiglas
9⅜ × 23¼ × 11⅝ inches (23.8 × 59.1 × 30.3 cm)
Produced by Braun AG, Frankfurt, Germany
K2010.240

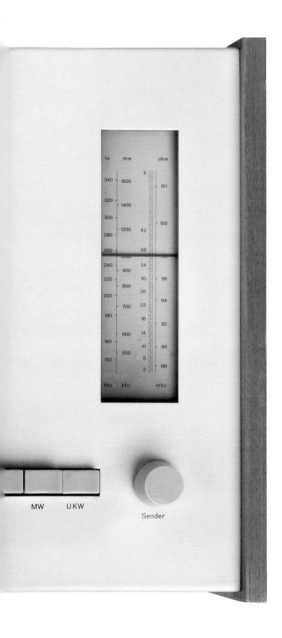

Office interior with *Phonosuper SK5*, from Braun promotional booklet, c. 1960

Max Bill
(1908–1994)
Kitchen clock with timer
Designed 1956–1957

Glazed earthenware, chromium-plated steel, glass
10¼ × 7¼ × 2¼ inches (26 × 18.5 × 5.7 cm)
Produced by Gebrüder Junghans AG, Schramberg, Germany
K2008.582

Arne Jacobsen
(1902–1971)
AJ flatware, model 660
Designed 1957

Stainless steel
Knife: 7¾ × ⅝ inches (19.7 × 1.6 cm)
Produced by A. Michelsen Silversmith,
Copenhagen, Denmark
K2010.125

Giò Ponti
(1891–1979)
Superleggera chair
Designed 1957

Ash, cane
32¾ × 15¾ × 17 inches (83.2 × 40 × 43.2 cm)
Produced by Cassina, S.p.A, Italy
Cooper Hewitt, Smithsonian Design Museum,
2013-54-1, gift of George R. Kravis II

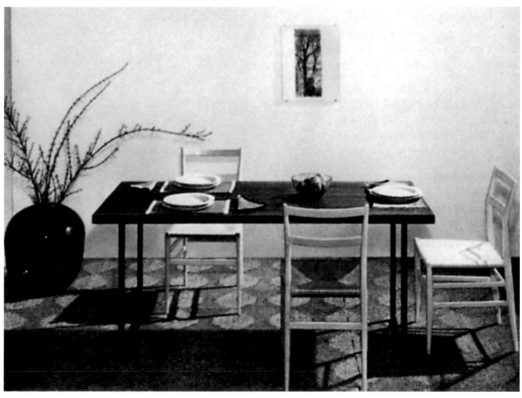

Dining room, Wohnhilfe exhibition, c. 1957, Basel, Switzerland

Verner Panton
(1926–1998)
Side chair
Designed c. 1960

Fiber-reinforced plastic
32 × 19¼ × 23¾ inches (81.3 × 48.9 × 60.3 cm)
Produced by Vitra GmbH for Herman Miller
Furniture Company, Zeeland, Michigan
K2009.5.1

Marianne Panton with Verner Panton–designed furnishings, photographed for the Danish magazine *Mobilia*, 1967

Eliot Noyes
(1910–1977)
Selectric typewriter
Designed 1961

Enameled aluminum, plastic
7½ × 21 × 15 inches (19.1 × 53.3 × 38.1 cm)
Produced by International Business Machines
Corporation (IBM), Armonk, New York
K2008.189

the

IBM

Selectric

a new kind of typewriter . . .

a new way to write!

The IBM Selectric is unlike any other typewriter you've ever seen! ■ It has no typebars! ■ It has no moving paper carriage! ■ It extends new versatility to a broad range of typing applications. ■ The secret? The precision-engineered single-element pictured above. ■ No bigger than a golf ball, it does the work of a "basketful" of typebars—and then some. ■ Skimming across the paper (just as your hand does when you write), it prints faster than the eye can see. ■ This full size office typewriter offers many other exclusive features. For example, a unique storage system that actually remembers, when necessary, one character while another is being printed . . . a single-unit ribbon cartridge that can be changed cleanly in seconds. ■ And that's not all. Want to change type style? Simple, with the Selectric! Slip off one typing element and click another type style in its place. ■ Ask your IBM representative to demonstrate the versatility of the IBM Selectric in your office. We think you will agree that this newest development from IBM research is an exciting addition to the IBM Typewriter line. **IBM**

Marco Zanuso
(1916–2001)
Richard Sapper
(born 1932)
Algol 11 portable
television
Designed 1964

Plastic, chromium-plated metal
9 × 12⅛ × 10¼ inches (22.9 × 30.8 × 26 cm)
Produced by Brionvega, S.p.A., Milan, Italy
K2011.27

Gino Valle
(1923–2003)
Monumental wall clock
Designed c. 1965

Enameled aluminum, glass
13 × 23 × 6¾ inches (33 × 58.4 × 17.1 cm)
Produced by Solari & C., Udine, Italy
K2012.56

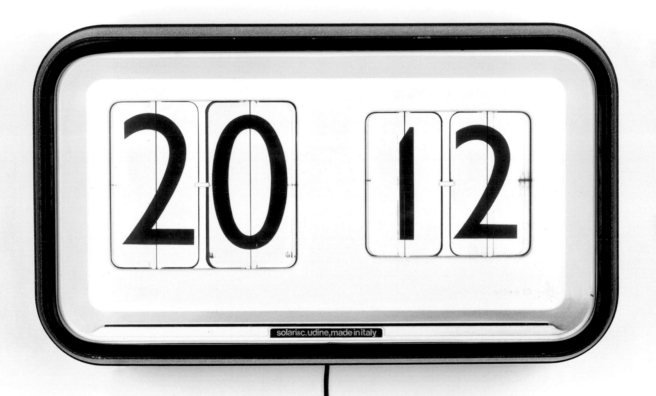

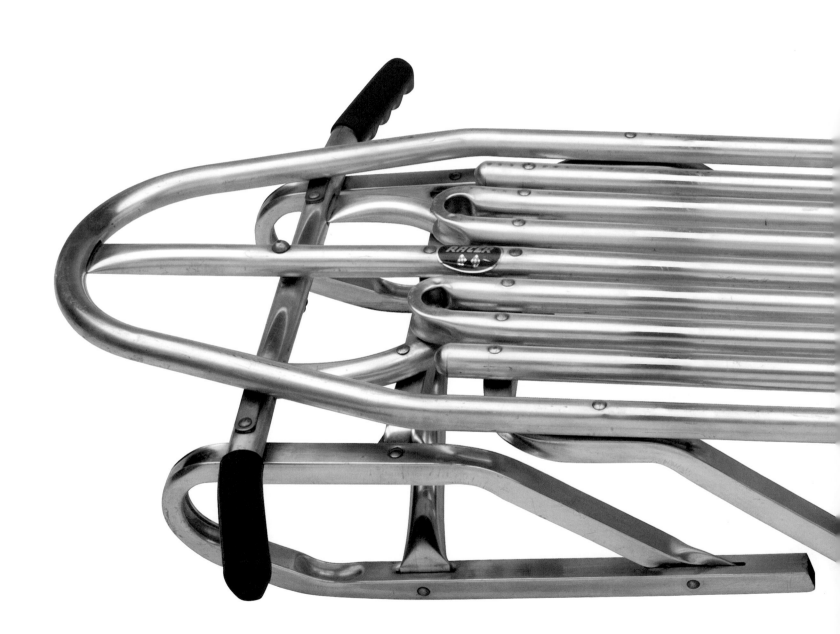

Bertram Lesser
(born 1924)
Morton I. Thomas
Racer sled
Designed c. 1965

Aluminum, plastic
7½ × 48 × 24¾ inches (19 × 122 × 63 cm)
Produced by Duralite, Passaic, New Jersey
K2010.131.1

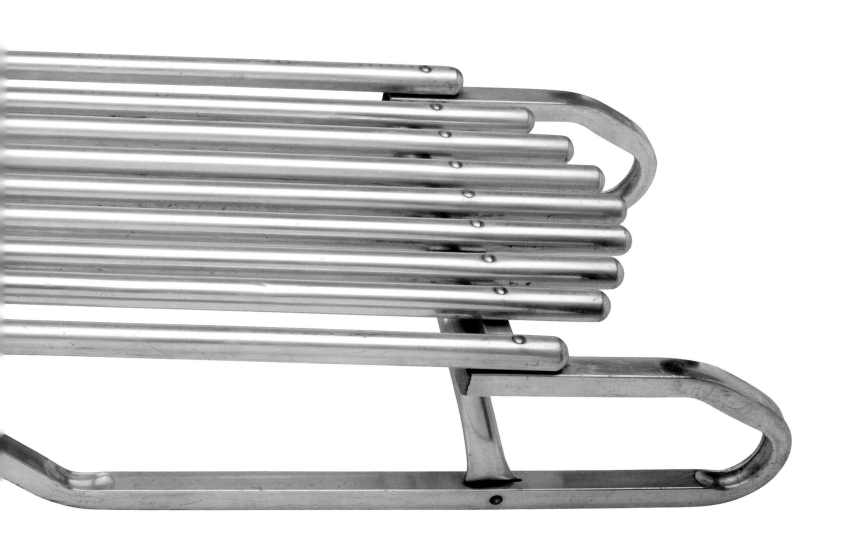

Alexander Girard
(1907–1993)
Lounge chair,
model 66310
Designed c. 1965

Cotton, wool, and nylon upholstery, vinyl,
plywood, aluminum
26 × 40½ × 29 inches (66 × 102.9 × 73.7 cm)
Produced by Herman Miller Furniture
Company, Zeeland, Michigan, for Braniff
International Airways
Cooper Hewitt, Smithsonian Design Museum,
2013-37-1, gift of George R. Kravis II in honor
of Caroline Baumann

Alexander Girard, club lounge for Braniff International Airways, Dallas Love Field, Texas,
from Braniff 1965 annual report

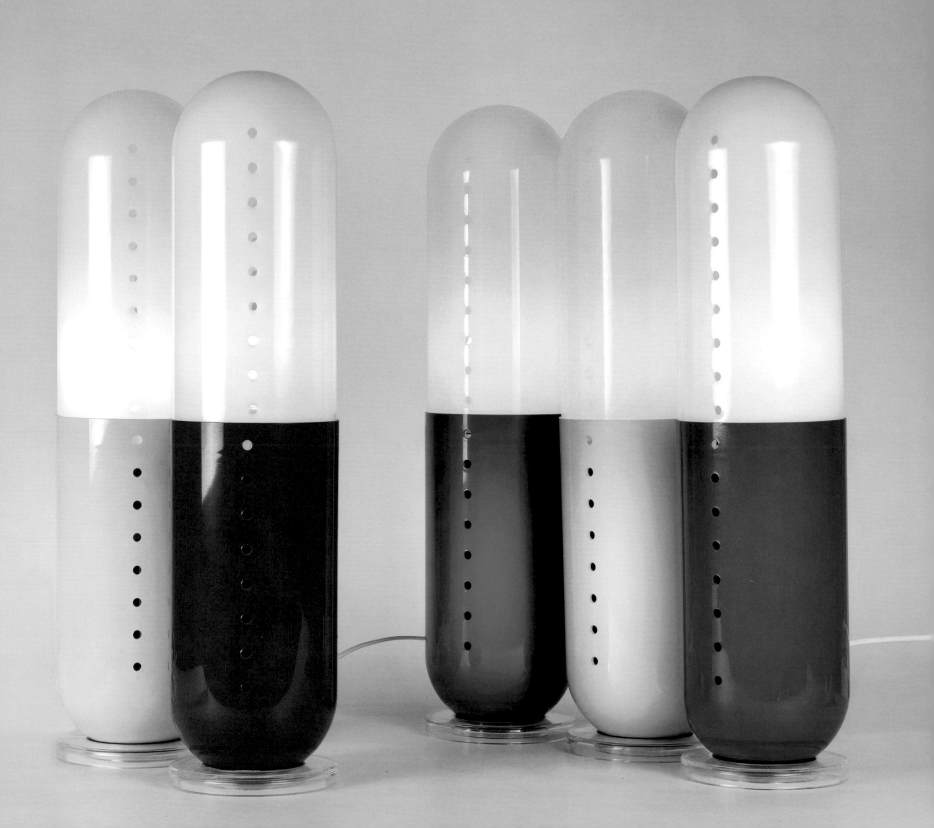

C. Emanuele Ponzio
(born 1923)
Cesare Casati
(born 1936)
Five *Pillola* lamps
Designed 1968

ABS plastic, acrylic
Each: 21¾ × 5⅛ × 5⅛ inches (55.2 × 13 × 13 cm)
Produced by Studio D.A. and Nia Ponteur,
Bergamo, Italy
K2014.22

Mario Bellini
(born 1935)
Pop Automatic record
player, model GA 45
Designed 1968

ABS plastic, metal
8⅝ × 7¾ × 3¼ inches (21.9 × 19.7 × 8.3 cm)
Produced by Minerva, Milan, Italy
K2008.477

Ettore Sottsass
(1917–2007)
Summa 19
adding machine
Designed 1970

Plastic, enameled metal
4⅛ × 10⅞ × 8⅛ inches (10.5 × 27.5 × 20.5 cm)
Produced by Ing. C. Olivetti & C., S.p.A.,
Ivrea, Italy
K2013.3

Richard Sapper
(born 1932)
Minitimer kitchen timer
Designed 1971

Plastic
1⅛ × 2⅝ × 2⅝ inches (2.8 × 6.7 × 6.7 cm)
Produced by Ritz-Italora, Milan, Italy
K2008.9.1

JVC
HIGH
MAX
LOW
TONE
AFC FM AM
TUNING
IC SOLID STATE
FUNCTION
T V
RADIO
POWER
O N
OFF

**International
Industrial Design**
Television and radio
Designed 1972

Styrol resin, aluminum, chromium-plated
steel, glass
Closed: 12¼ × 11½ × 11¼ inches
(31 × 29.2 × 28.7 cm)
Produced by Japan Victor Company,
Tokyo, Japan
K2011.2

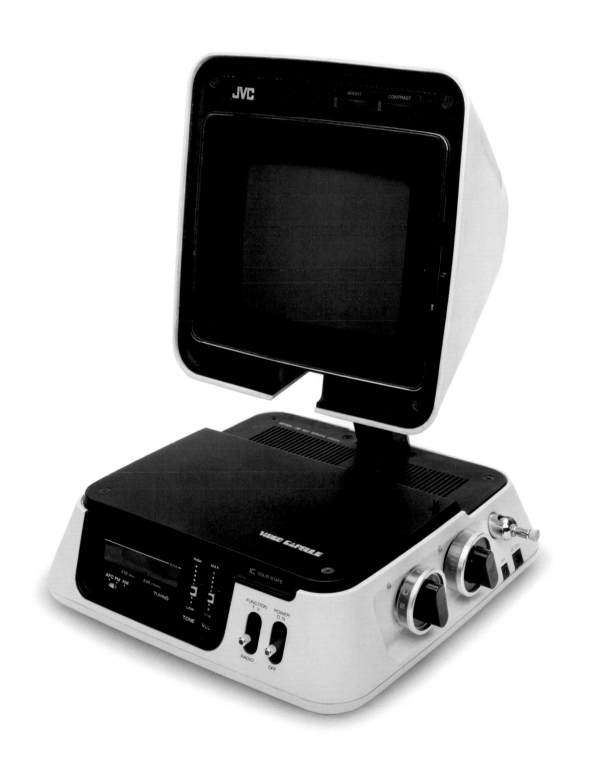

Frank O. Gehry
(born 1929)
Wiggle side chair
Designed 1972

Cardboard, Masonite
33½ × 24 × 16¼ inches (85.1 × 61 × 41.3 cm)
Produced by Easy Edges, Inc.,
New York, New York
K2012.57

Carlo Scarpa
(1906–1978)
Pitcher
Designed c. 1978

Silver
8¾ × 6 × 4½ inches (22.2 × 15.2 × 11.4 cm)
Produced by Cleto Munari, Venice, Italy
K2010.332

Javier Mariscal
(born 1950)
Pepe Cortés
(born 1946)
Hilton serving cart
Designed 1981

Enameled metal, glass, rubber
31½ × 56¼ × 17¾ inches (80 × 143 × 45 cm)
Produced for Memphis, Milan, Italy
K2011.208

Living room of Thomas Lear Grace and Lorry Parks Dudley, 1980s, Houston, Texas, showing *Hilton* serving cart and *Carlton* bookcase by Ettore Sottsass

Paul Rand
(1914–1996)
Eye Bee M poster
Designed 1982

Offset lithograph
36 × 24 inches (91.5 × 61 cm)
Produced by International Business Machines
Corporation (IBM), New York, New York
K2012.70

Masanori Umeda
(born 1941)
Ginza cabinet
Designed 1982

Painted wood, plastic laminate,
chromium-plated metal
68⅞ × 59 × 16½ inches (175 × 150 × 42 cm)
Produced for Memphis, Milan, Italy
K2013.171

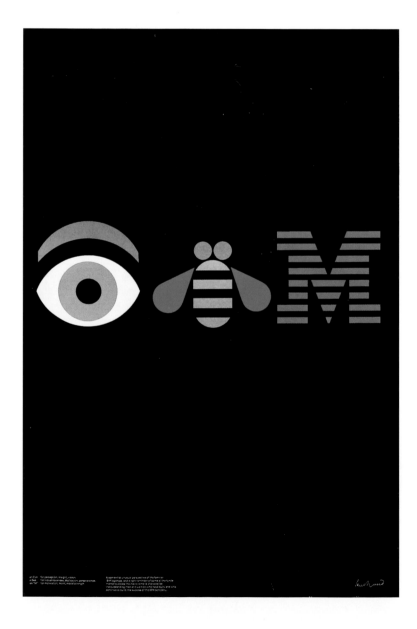

Shiro Kuramata
(1934–1991)
Kyoto table
Designed 1983

Terrazzo, chromium-plated steel
28 × 23¼ × 23¼ inches (71.1 × 59.1 × 59.1 cm)
Produced by Ishimaru Company, Ltd., Japan,
for Memphis, Milan, Italy
K2008.340

Mario Bellini
(born 1935)
ET Personal 55
typewriter
Designed 1985–1986

ABS polymer
4⅞ × 16⅛ × 13 inches (12.4 × 41 × 33 cm)
Produced by Ing. C. Olivetti & C., S.p.A.,
Ivrea, Italy
K2013.13

Michael Graves
(1934–2015)
The Little Dripper
tea service
Designed 1987

Enameled and gilt porcelain
Teapot: 8⅞ × 10⅜ × 6¾ inches
(22.5 × 26.5 × 17 cm)
Produced for Swid Powell,
New York, New York
K2010.147

Alberto Meda
(born 1945)
Light Light armchair
Designed c. 1987

Carbon fiber, Nomex composite
honeycomb
29¼ × 21¾ × 19½ inches
(74.3 × 55.2 × 49.5 cm)
Produced by Alias, S.p.A., Bergamo, Italy
K2012.102

Marc Newson
(born 1963)
Embryo chair
Designed 1988

Neoprene, chromium-plated steel, aluminum
31½ × 33½ × 31½ inches
(80 × 85.1 × 80 cm)
Produced by Idée, Tokyo, Japan
K2008.339

David Hockney
(born 1937)
Swimming Pool carpet
Designed 1988

Tufted wool
122 × 78¾ inches (310 × 200 cm)
Produced by Vorwerk & Co.,
Wuppertal, Germany
K2014.23

Massimo Iosa-Ghini
(born 1959)
Faro table lamp
Designed 1988

Chromium-plated steel, aluminum, glass
16 × 8⅞ × 6½ inches (40.5 × 22.5 × 16.5 cm)
Produced for Memphis, Milan, Italy
K2009.1

Ingo Maurer
(born 1932)
One from the Heart
table lamp
Designed 1989

Metal, plastic, mirror glass
37⅜ × 15¾ inches (95 × 40 cm)
Produced by Ingo Maurer GmbH,
Munich, Germany
K2008.95.1

Shigeru Uchida
(born 1943)
Dear Morris clock
Designed 1989

Lacquered wood, glass
53¼ × 9½ × 9½ inches (135.3 × 24.1 × 24.1 cm)
Produced by Morphos, Bergamo, Italy
K2010.163

Shigeru Uchida, *Dear Vera 1* and *2*, 1991, produced by Alessi

Philippe Starck
(born 1949)
W.W. stool
Designed 1990

Enameled aluminum
38½ × 21¼ × 22⅝ inches (97.8 × 54 × 57.5 cm)
Produced by Vitra AG, Birsfelden, Switzerland
K2009.31

Philippe Starck, Felix Restaurant and Oyster Bar, Peninsula Hotel, Hong Kong, 1994

Tom Dixon
(born 1959)
Pylon chair
Designed 1991

Painted steel
50 × 27 × 21 inches (127 × 68.6 × 53.3 cm)
Produced by Cappellini, S.p.A., Milan, Italy
K2010.123

Born in Tunisia, Tom Dixon moved to London in 1963, where he studied at the Chelsea School of Art. He was one of the "metal basher" artists, who employed the look of scrap metal roughly welded together. Over time, Dixon moved to more organic forms in metal and rattan and then to dematerialized designs such as the *Pylon* chair. The symmetrical, architectonic design consists of an assembly of open wire triangles crowned by a hovering backrest. Initially made and sold in a limited edition by Dixon's own company, the chair was put into production by Cappellini in 1992.

Shigeru Ban
(born 1957)
Carta bench
Designed 1998

Cardboard tubes, plywood, fabric
14½ × 72⅞ × 2⅝ inches (37 × 185 × 60 cm)
Produced by Cappellini, S.p.A., Milan, Italy
K2010.71

Shigeru Ban, interior, Wall-less House, Nagano, Japan, 1997, with variation of *Carta* bench

Mathias Bengtsson
(born 1971)
Slice armchair
Designed 1999

Laminated plywood
31 × 34½ × 32 inches
(78.7 × 87.6 × 81.3 cm)
Produced by Mathias Bengtsson Studio,
Stockholm, Sweden
K2011.94

Mathias Bengtsson began his career as part of Panic, a group of young Danish furniture designers. In 1996, he moved to London to study at the Royal College of Art under Ron Arad. *Slice* was developed in a studio founded by Bengtsson and his fellow graduates. Each chair comprises 388 sheets of laser-cut three-millimeter plywood glued together, employing advanced technology and crafts-manship to create a sculptural form. The design was also produced in limited numbers in aluminum.

Ross Lovegrove
(born 1958)
Agaricon table lamp
Designed 2001

Polycarbonate plastic, aluminum
18⅞ × 16⅛ × 16⅛ inches (28 × 41 × 41 cm)
Produced by Luceplan, Milan, Italy
K2012.94

Office interior with *Agaricon* lamp

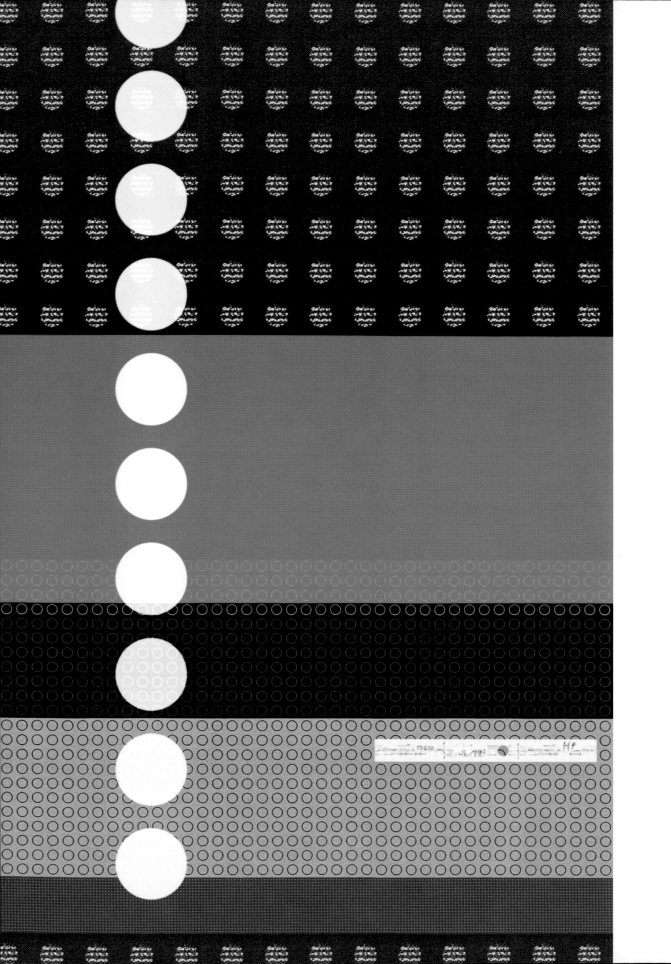

Hella Jongerius
(born 1963)
Repeat Dot Print textile
Designed 2001

Cotton, polyester, rayon
87½ × 56½ inches (222.3 × 143.5 cm)
Produced by Maharam, New York, New York
K2008.233

Maharam showroom, NeoCon trade fair, 2002, Chicago, Illinois

Konstantin Grcic
(born 1965)
Chair_One chair
Designed 2004

Enameled aluminum, aluminum
33 × 22 × 24 inches (83.8 × 55.9 × 61 cm)
Produced by Magis, Torre di Mosto, Italy
K2010.78

Jasper Morrison
(born 1959)
Toaster
Designed 2004

Polypropylene, stainless steel
7⅝ × 15⅛ × 4⅜ inches (19.5 × 38.5 × 11 cm)
Produced by Rowenta, United Kingdom
K2008.290

Yves Béhar
(born 1967)
Leaf Light lamp
Designed 2005

Aluminum, plastic
20⅛ × 18¾ × 8⅝ inches (51 × 47.5 × 22 cm)
Produced by Herman Miller Inc.,
Zeeland, Michigan
K2008.217

Swiss-born Yves Béhar founded the industrial design firm Fuseproject in 1999. He is known for creating products that are sustainable and meet the needs of the world's poor and disadvantaged. *Leaf Light* explores sustainability through LED lighting, which uses 40 percent less energy than fluorescent. The design is the first lighting product for Herman Miller, a company known for its modern furniture. The gently twisted aluminum composition, which incorporates a hinged arm, balances delicately on a circular base, evoking the aesthetic presence of a sculpture posed on a pedestal.

Jonathan Ive
(born 1967)
Apple Design Team
iPod Nano 2G and *iPod Shuffle 2G* MP3 players
Designed 2006

Polycarbonate, ABS plastic
Nano: 3⅜ × 1 × ⅜ inches (8.5 × 2.5 × 0.8 cm)
Produced by Apple Computer, Inc., Cupertino, California
K2008.204.1–2

Susan Alinsangan, TBWA\Chiat\Day, advertising posters, 2006

Alexander Taylor
(born 1975)
Two *Grip* flashlights
Designed 2012

Silicone, rubber, LED light source
Each: 6 × 3⅜ × 3⅜ inches (15.3 × 9 × 9 cm)
Produced by PRAXIS, United Kingdom, for the
Conran Shop's RED exhibition, London Design
Festival, September 2012
K2012.97.1–2

British designer Alexander Taylor was inspired by BMX
bicycle grips to create this silicone and rubber flashlight. The
wide circular head surrounding the bright LED allows it to
stand easily. The sculptural form is comfortable to grip and
offers aesthetic and tactile pleasure. The flashlight was
produced in a broad range of colors; the red version
was conceived especially for the Conran Shop's RED
exhibition at the 2012 London Design Festival.

Acknowledgments

This book is the result of the dedicated work of many talented people. We are indebted to Penny Sparke for her scholarship, both in her curatorial role in the selection of objects from the Kravis Design Center and for her thoughtful essay on industrial design. Tulsa-based Shane Culpepper demonstrated his visual sensibility in capturing the essential aesthetic of many of the objects in the Kravis Design Center. We thank him for his prodigious work under tight deadlines.

Several institutions supplied images for this book. We recognize Jennifer Belt, Associate Permissions Director, Art Resource, New York; Tatiana Tonizzo, Head of Brand Communications, Cappellini, Milan; Sarah D. Coffin, Curator and Head, Product Design and Decorative Arts Department, and Allison Hale, Digital Imaging Specialist, Cooper Hewitt, Smithsonian Design Museum, New York; Dr. Gerti Draxler, Dorotheum, Vienna; Amy Auscherman, Corporate Archivist, Herman Miller, Zeeland, Michigan; Tascha Mae Horowitz, Manager of Photography, and Robin Lawrence, Rights and Reproductions Assistant, Indianapolis Museum of Art; Angela Guevara, Ingo Maurer LLC, New York; Elizabeth Portanova, Los Angeles Modern Auctions; Christie Boyle, Chrysanthemum Partners, for Luceplan, Milan; Sara Sheth, Marketing, Maharam, New York; Lorry Dudley, The Modern Archive, Easton, Maryland; Bradley Goad, Administrator, Design Department, Phillips, New York; Anthony Barnes, Graphic/Web Designer, Rago Arts and Auction Center, Lambertville, New Jersey; Kit Wallace, Administrator, 20th Century Design, Sotheby's, New York; Angéline Dazé, Registrar, Stewart Program for Modern Design, Montreal; Lauren Kristin, Communications Department, Swann Auction Galleries, New York; and Michael Jefferson and Todd Simeone, Wright, Chicago.

We are grateful to the individuals and institutions who have offered information and resources. Paul Galloway, The Museum of Modern Art, New York; Josef Strasser, Die Neue Sammlung, Munich; and Lisanne Dickson, Treadway/Toomey Auctions, Oak Park, Illinois, provided valuable information about objects. Design curator R. Craig Miller and architect Wendy Joseph have been generous with their guidance and support.

The beautiful design of this publication is the work of Rick Landers, Elizabeth Kelley, Terrence Sanchez, and Ken Carbone at the Carbone Smolan Agency, New York.

Special thanks go to Kate Clark in the office of David A. Hanks and Associates, New York, for research and obtaining photographs and permissions, as well as editing and myriad details. We were fortunate to have Andrea Monfried manage the project and edit the text. We are grateful to Tommy Anderson for coordinating logistics at the Kravis Design Center.

Rizzoli has been an enthusiastic partner in this project, particularly publisher Charles Miers, who first approached George Kravis about a book. We also thank Margaret Rennolds Chace, Associate Publisher, Skira Rizzoli Publications, and Monica A. Davis, Rizzoli International Publications.

Finally, and most important, this book would not exist without collector George R. Kravis II, whose extraordinary commitment to industrial design we celebrate in these pages.

David A. Hanks
Curator, Kravis Design Center

Index of Names

Photography Credits

Bauhaus-Archiv Berlin: 23, 27
Cooper Hewitt, Smithsonian Design Museum: 32–33, 48, 128
Shane Culpepper, Tulsa: cover, 2, 5, 6, 14, 20–21, 22, 24, 25, 26, 28, 29, 34, 35, 36, 37, 38, 39, 40, 42, 46, 47, 50, 51, 52, 53, 54–55, 56, 59, 60–61, 62, 63, 64, 65, 66, 66–67, 70, 71, 72, 76–77, 78–79, 80, 83, 84, 85, 86, 90–91, 94, 96–97, 100, 102, 106, 108–109, 110, 113, 114–115, 116, 117, 120, 122, 124, 126–127, 131, 132, 133, 134–135, 137, 142, 143, 144–145, 147, 149, 155, 156–157, 164, 165, 168, 170–171
David A. Hanks & Associates Archive: 115
Dorotheum: 130, 141, 148
Front Design: 16 top
General Motors Media Archive: 13
Getty Images: 12 top (Hulton Archive), 169 (photograph by Justin Sullivan)
Herman Miller Archives: 88–89, 93, 101, 167
Indianapolis Museum of Art: 8 (gift of George R. Kravis II in honor of Craig Miller, 2012.76A–B, imamuseum.org), 30–31, 74
Ingo Maurer LLC: 150
©J. Paul Getty Trust, Getty Research Institute, Los Angeles: 105 (photograph by Julius Shulman, 2004.R.10)
Eileen MacAvery Kane: 16 bottom
Kravis Design Archives: 12 bottom, 55, 75, 81, 123
Photograph Courtesy of Los Angeles Modern Auctions (LAMA): 138
Courtesy Luceplan: 160, 161
Maharam: 162, 163
©The Modern Archive: 139 (photograph by Hickey Robertson, 1983)
©The Museum of Modern Art/Licensed by SCALA/Art Resource, New York: 11, 43, 98–99
Rago Arts and Auction Center: 69
Courtesy of Phillips: 146
Courtesy Shigeru Ban Architects: 157 (photograph by Hiroyuki Hirai; wb form in Switzerland is producing the bench as of 2015)
Courtesy of Swann Auction Galleries: 45, 140
Matthew Tyas: 17
Courtesy Uchida Design Inc.: 151 left (photograph by Takayuki Ogawa)
Verner Panton Design: 121
©Victoria and Albert Museum, London: 10 bottom, 15 top
Wright, Chicago: 15 bottom, 44, 88, 92, 95, 104, 112, 118, 125, 136, 151 right, 152, 158

First published in the United States of America in 2016 by
SKIRA RIZZOLI PUBLICATIONS, INC.
300 Park Avenue South, New York, NY 10010
www.rizzoliusa.com

Library of Congress Cataloguing-in-Publication Data
Kravis Design Center (Tulsa, Okla.)
100 designs for a modern world / foreword by George R. Kravis II ; introduction by Penny Sparke, Rizzoli/Kravis Design Center.
pages   cm
Selected pieces from the Kravis Design Center, Tulsa, Oklahoma.
Includes index.
ISBN 978-0-8478-4832-4
1. Industrial design—Pictorial works. 2. Product design—Pictorial works. I. Kravis, George R., II, writer of foreword. II. Sparke, Penny, writer of introduction. III. Rizzoli International Publications. IV. Title. V. Title: One hundred designs for a modern world.
TS171.6.K73 2016
658.5'752—dc23   2015021677

Designed by Carbone Smolan Agency

Printed and bound in China

2016 2017 2018 2019 2020 / 10 9 8 7 6 5 4 3 2 1